Decorative Quilling

Pansies (see page 27)

Decorative Quilling

50 NEW DESIGNS

Trees Tra and Malinda Johnston

Kangaroo Press

Designer: Karel van Laar, de Bilt.
Photography: Studio Koppelman, Maarssen.
Drawings: Malinda Johnston.

English Translation © 1993 Kangaroo Press

Reprinted in 1993, 1994, 1995, 1996, 1997, 1998, 1999 twice,
2001, 2002
This edition first published in 1992 by Kangaroo Press
an imprint of Simon & Schuster (Australia) Pty Limited
20 Barcoo Street, East Roseville NSW 2069
Printed in Hong Kong through Colorcraft Ltd

ISBN 0 86417 560 4

Contents

Foreword 7
Basic shapes 8
Modern wall plaque with gilded paper 14
Flower varieties 16
Flower alphabet 18
Panda 25
Pansies 27
Poppies 28
Fantastic bird 30
Exotic flowers 30
Christmas bells and stars 31
Picture alphabet 34
Flower basket 40
Oval cards 42
Birth announcements 44
Gift tags 46
Christmas cards 48

Small gift tags, very easy to make

Foreword

On the initiative of Pieter van der Wolk and our publishers Cantecleer BV a meeting was arranged between me and Malinda Johnston, who lives in Highlandville, Missouri, in the United States. My reception by Malinda in the United States was very welcoming. Our common interest in quilling was a strong basis for a friendship.

For almost two weeks I was a guest of the Johnston family in their home, two weeks in which we worked hard on the ideas and designs for this book. Of course, not all the designs were finished in those two weeks—some of them were partly formed and finished later.

Working in another country with a long tradition of quilling led me to a lot of new ideas, many of which are incorporated here. We hope that these ideas in their turn will give your imagination a boost and lead you to enjoy quilling for a long time.

Trees Tra

Basic shapes

Quilling designs are all made up from rolled coils, which can be worked into innumerable shapes. All the shapes used in the book are shown on the next few pages. The major distinction is between open coils and closed coils.

Open coils

To make an open coil, roll the paper strips from one or both ends; rolling clockwise or anticlockwise will create different effects. The shapes can be changed by glueing the coils together, lengthening the straight piece or folding the straight piece. The length of the strip of paper will determine the size of the shape.

Examples of open coils

1 *Single open coil*
Roll the paper strip from one end into a coil, leaving approximately 2 cm (¾") free.

2 *V shape*
Fold the paper strip in half and curl both ends outwards away from each other.

3 *Closed V shape*
The same as the V shape, but glue ends together.

4 *Open heart shape*
Fold paper strip in half, curl both ends inwards towards each other.

5 *Closed heart shape*
Fold paper strip in half, curl both ends towards each other, glue both coils together.

6 *Scroll*
Roll both ends towards each other, leaving middle straight or slightly bent.

7 *Letter S*
Curl coils away from each other.

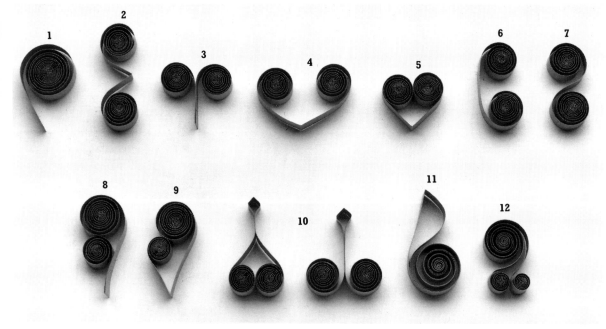

Basic shapes: open coils

8 *Double coils*
Fold the strip of paper, leaving one end longer than the other. Roll both ends in the same direction.

9 *Opposite coil*
Same as for double coil, but roll the short end towards the inside.

10 *Double coil with open window, rolled to the outside or inside*
Fold the paper strip in the middle and roll both ends to the outside or the inside, leaving several centimetres from the centre unfolded. Apply glue 1 cm (⅜″) below the fold and apply pressure to the fold, forming a window.

11 *Half a harp*
Fold a strip in half and roll both ends together. The inside of the strip will need less paper than the outside, thus forming a loop below the fold.

12 *Triple coil*
Fold a strip in half, roll ends one by one to the outside or the inside to approximately halfway, then roll the double strip back to meet itself.

Closed coils

The closed coil is made in a slightly different way. The paper strip is torn, which creates a slightly rough edge which is easier to glue. Roll the strip of paper leaving a small piece at the end. At the very end apply a little glue with a toothpick. Holding the coil between thumb and forefinger attach the free end to the coil with a loop. The length of the loop determines the size of the coil. Once the glue has set lay the coil down and it will spring open. If it fails to open it probably means that a small amount of glue has found its way into the coil. This can be rectified by running a pin through the coil. The coil can then be pressed into any shape with the fingers or fingernails.

Examples of closed coils

13 *Tight coil/tight circle*
Roll the strip of paper as tightly as you can, and glue the end.
Grape roll (a variation of the tight coil)
Roll a tight circle and gently push the

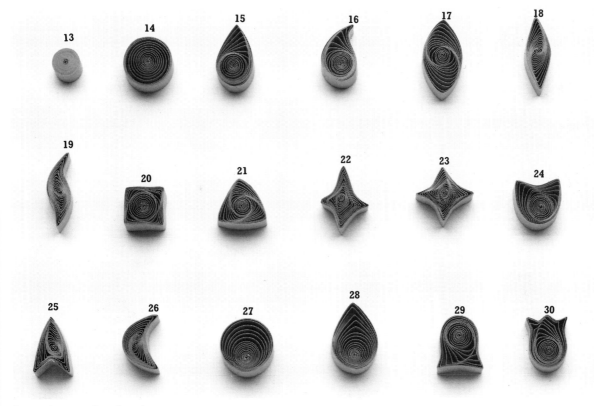

Basic shapes: closed coils

centre out to make a conical roll. Spread a thin layer of glue on the inside surface so that the roll will retain its shape.

14 *Loose coil*
Roll the strip leaving a small straight piece at the end. Apply glue with a toothpick and attach the end with a loop to the coil. The larger the size of the loop the looser the coil.

15 *Teardrop*
Make a loose coil. Hold the centre carefully with one finger or a pin, with the other hand hold the side of the coil. Pull the centre towards the edge and pinch into a point with thumb and first finger.

16 *Flame*
Make a teardrop by pinching the end and bending it in the opposite direction to the circle.

17 *Oval (marquise)*
Make a loose coil and flatten slightly between the thumb and first finger.

18 *Diamond*
Same as the oval but pinch both ends sharply.

19 *Leaf*
Same as for oval, but pinch the ends with one hand twisting away from you and one hand twisting towards you.

20 *Square*
Make a loose coil, squeeze with thumb and forefinger at both ends, at the same time forming a square.

21 *Triangle*
Make a loose coil, pressing coil with finger and thumb of one hand and finger of the other hand at the same time.

22 *Holly leaf*
Make a loose coil, press with the nails of both the thumbs and the forefingers. Make sure the coil has been wound very loosely to ensure you have enough room. This shape does not need to be very even.

23 *Star*
The same as for the holly leaf, but making sure the points are even.

24 *Flower petal (bunny ears)*
Make a loose coil and press with the fingernail to make a rounded indentation at the top of the coil.

25 *Arrow*
Make a flower petal and pinch a sharp indentation at the bottom of the petal.

26 *Half moon (crescent)*
Make a loose coil. Press the coil flat and pull both points to one side.

27 *Loose coil with offset centre*
Make a loose coil and pull the centre to one side, applying glue to the back of the coil. Let glue dry before continuing to shape.

28 *Leaf shape with offset centre*
Similar to loose coil, but when glue has dried pinch top into leaf shape.
These last two shapes are easier to make using the quilling template.

29 *Bell*
Make a flower petal, pinching the ends and twisting them to the outside.

30 *Tulip*
Make a bell; while pinching the ends press in towards the centre thus making an extra point.

Freeform shapes

Strips of paper can simply be folded or bent to any shape desired and then glued to the background. It is possible to make leaves, grass or birds with freeform strips. Glueing strips of paper to the background can make a frame for a design.

31 *Stretched leaf*
Two strips of paper of uneven length glued together at the ends will make a stretched leaf.

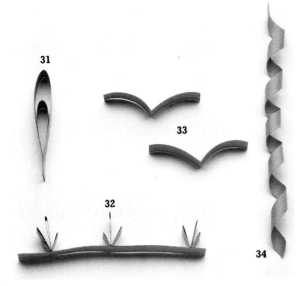

Freeform shapes

Basic shapes for extending designs

32 *Grass*
By folding a strip of paper in small sections it is possible to create the illusion of grass. Glue this to a flat strip of paper and it will stand up.

33 *Birds*
Take small strips of paper, fold in the centre, and slightly bend the sides.

34 *Spirals*
Wind strips of paper diagonally around a toothpick or a satay stick.

Extending basic shapes

1 *Open loose coil with offset centre*
Using a quilling template make a loose coil with an offset centre. Apply glue using a pin. When the glue is dry, remove the pin by turning in a circular motion. Lift the coil out of the template. With pointed scissors cut the outside layer or layers of paper. The part of the coil that remains uncut assumes a fan shape.

2 *Open leaf shape with offset centre*
As in the previous shape, make a loose coil in the quilling template and shape it into a leaf (number 28). With scissors cut one or more layers of paper at the fold.

3 *Loose coil with offset centre and two loops*
A difficult shape to give a name to, but it is made as follows. On the quilling template make a coil with an offset centre. With a second pin press several of the paper rolls together, directly opposite the first pin. This becomes a figure eight shape. Apply glue to the second pin and spread the glue approximately 2 mm (¹⁄₁₆"). When the glue has dried remove the pins and lift the coil out of the template. Cut the glued strips so that the glue holds the loops together.

4 *Centre-cut strip*
To give an extra dimension to your work, cut a strip of paper lengthwise down the middle. Both sides can be rolled into a loose coil, leaving one end lying loosely against the background.

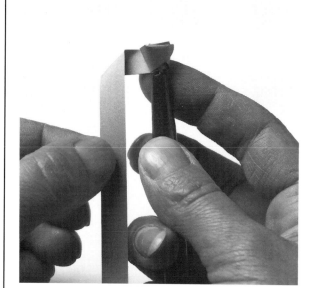
Making a rose

5 *Fish*
From one strip of paper make a closed coil. Pull the centre completely to one side and with the thumb and forefinger of the other hand form the opposite end into a point. Holding the pointed end apply glue to the side of the coil, directly in front of the bulge. Let the glue dry while holding the shape.

6 *Holly-leaves* (six pointed)
Using a 24 cm (9½") strip, make a loose circle. Make a sharp oval. Take it with the point between thumb and finger and shape it to a square. Take the square with the flat sides between your fingers and shape it again. Pull out the points one by one and round the flat sides a bit.

7 *Folded roses*
You need a slotted tool to do this. Use paper 5 or 7 mm (³⁄₁₆" OR ¼") wide. The end of the paper is held securely in the slot which makes it easier to maintain the tension while folding the rose. Slip the paper into the slot and begin rolling on the tool to form centre. Next fold the paper toward you at a right angle. Roll the paper on the tool, allowing the top edge to flare out, until the flare is on the top. Keep the bottom edge tight to the tool. Repeat this

several times. Glue the end to the underside of the rose.

8 *Fringed leaves*
Cut out leaves from a 5 or 7 mm (³⁄₁₆" OR ¼") wide strip. Fringe edge to the centre and curl slightly. These leaves can also be made using a fringer.

9 *Loops*
Cut two lengths of 10 mm (³⁄₈") width paper. Overlap and glue the ends to form a tight pointed roll. Trim the ends. To make the loops equal, draw two lines on paper at a 45° angle. The smaller the angle the longer the point will be. Place the strip along one line, turn it and lead the end along the other line. Pull until the point is exactly in the angle, and glue (see picture).

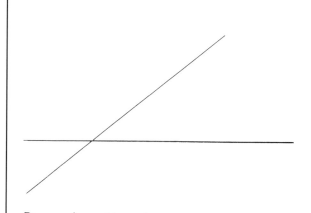
Diagram for making a loop

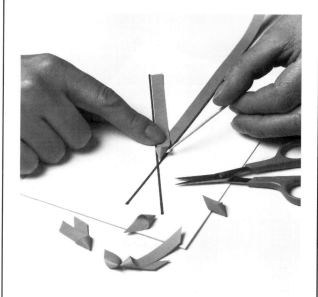
Making a loop

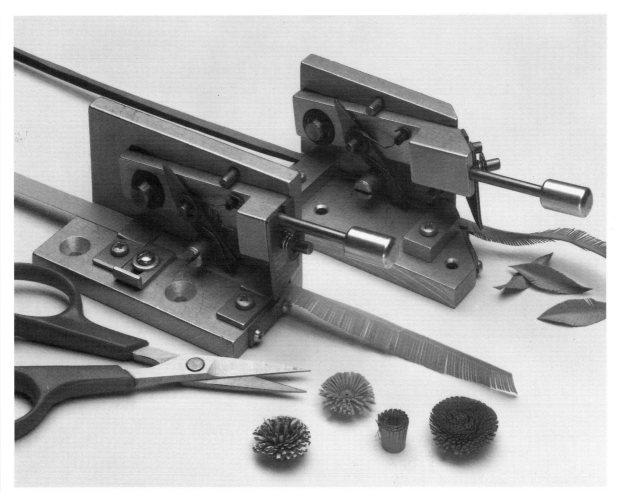

Fringing machines like these take the pain out of making fringed flowers and leaves

Fringed flowers and leaves

Flowers
For making fringed flowers it is better to use 5 or 7 mm (³⁄₁₆″ or ¼″) strips. Make perpendicular cuts in the strip 1 mm (¹⁄₃₂″) apart, leaving a 'spine' 1 mm (¹⁄₃₂″) wide. Make a tight circle. Bow the fringed edge away from the centre. You can give the flowers a centre by glueing a 3 mm (⅛″) strip to the wider fringed one. Begin rolling on the narrower strip. Rolling two different colours gives a multi-coloured flower.

Leaves
Fringed leaves are cut from a wider strip or a piece of green paper. Cut slantwise from the edge to the centre for about 2 mm (¹⁄₁₆″). The leaves can be curved slightly and gracefully.

Cutting many leaves and flowers this way is very tiring. Those of you who do a lot of quilling may wish to invest in a very handy tool that takes over the cutting for you. The first fringer in the photograph (model 90) cuts strips at an angle of 90° for flowers. The fringer at the back (model 45) cuts a folded strip at an angle of 45° to make beautiful leaves.

Modern wall plaque with gilded paper

This modern wall decoration is made of curved and milled strips. (Instructions for milling are given below.) The curved strips (15) are 24.5 cm (9¾") long and glued together at one end. To curve a group of strips, hold the strips in both hands. Bow the strips with one hand, while you relax the other hand. Then grip the strips firmly with the relaxed hand and bow them in the opposite direction. Repeating this movement several times will cause the strips to curve in a uniform fashion.

When you like the shape they are making, you will have to fix it. Fix the strips with pins on your quilling board and glue the ends where the strips touch each other. Let the glue dry before you proceed.

When you have enough of these shapes, you can glue them onto a framed

---

Continued from page 16.

20: Glue 6 teardrops (16 cm) to a tight circle (12 cm).
Glue about 20 loose scrolls (1.5 cm × 1.5 mm) over the centre tight circle.
21: Make three multi-pointed holly leaves (15 cm).
Make three grape rolls (15 cm), and glue together.
22: Make 6 teardrops (18 cm) and glue them together in pairs.
Between each pair of teardrops glue 1 oval (3 cm).
Glue stems on top of the flowers.

The green leaves with the flowers can be made of different shapes (leaves, teardrops, vines) or cut from wider strips.

background in an interesting composition. Parts that project into the frame area can be cut away.

Now position the milled strips. Over the spot where the curved shapes join you now fix an elaborate round shape. First, make a tight circle with a diameter of 2 cm (¾"), glue a milled strip around it and then a plain one. Repeat this until the circle has the desired diameter.

Milling paper strips

To make milled strips you need a Lego Technics system or something similar, with cogs that are not too deep or too sharp. Pass the strips of paper between the wheels, being careful not to exert pressure on the paper. Glue the milled strip to a plain strip of paper by applying glue only to the bumps, then gently pressing the milled strip to the flat strip of paper. Don't glue one milled strip to another milled strip, but always glue a flat strip between milled strips. Frames or outlines are strongest if made with milled edges. Two or three layers of milled and flat strips will make a sturdy frame.

Making a milled strip

Approx: 1.5 mm = ¹⁄₁₆"; 1.5 cm = ½"; 3 cm = 1¼"; 12 cm = 4½"; 15 cm = 6"; 16 cm = 6¼"; 18 cm = 7"

This wall decoration, using curved and milled strips, was made of gilded paper, which gives it a special touch

Flower varieties

Flowers are a source of inspiration for every lover of quilling. Such is the variety of shapes and colours that the possibilities for inspiration are almost inexhaustible.

1: 4 closed hearts (6 cm)
1 tight circle (3 cm) on the centre
Attach 2 fringed leaves to the flower.

2: 5 flower petals (bunny ears) (12 cm)
3 flower petals (bunny ears) (9 cm)
1 tight circle (4 cm) for the centre
Glue the five flower petals together first, then the three smaller ones on top with the points in the centre.

3: 1 tight circle (6 cm)
5 loose circles (6 cm)
1 V scroll

4: 4 grape rolls (12 cm)
3 ovals (12 cm)
1 strip (6 cm)

5: 9 flower petals (12 cm)
First glue 6 together, then 3, with the points in the centre. Add a 1 cm fringed strip in the centre.

6: 3 loose circles (12 cm)
1 tight circle (6 cm) on the top

7: 10 loops
Glue five loops with the points together on a small piece of paper. Then glue the other five with the loops in the centre.

8: *Fringed flowers*
Follow the instructions on page 13.
Vines
Fold a strip and roll a small piece from the fold, then pull back the inner strip.

9: 7 ovals (15 cm)
7 ovals (10 cm)
1 tight circle
Make two single flowers. Take the smaller in the palm of your hand and press the centre in, then glue it on the larger flower. Glue the tight circle in the centre.

10: Glue a teardrop (6 cm) in the centre of a V scroll (8 cm). Add a stem with 2 ovals (10 cm).

11: Make 3 cone shapes.
Glue 3 loose scrolls (2 cm × 1.5 mm) in each. Make three glued V scrolls (6, 8 and 12 cm) with a long stem. Glue the flowers between the V scrolls, and glue the stems together.

12: Punch 5 circles (or cut them) with a diameter of 7 mm. Glue them to overlap each other. Make the flower concave and glue a tight circle (4 cm × 1.5 mm) in the centre.

13: Glue 5 teardrops (12 cm) with the points together.
1 tight circle (6 cm) on the top.

14: Glue 5 light-coloured strips (8 cm) to 5 dark-coloured strips (3 cm). Starting from the light ends, make 5 flower petals and glue them to a tight circle (8 cm) of the darker colour.

15: Cut 2 cm pieces from 7 mm paper. Cut points or curves on one end. Notch the other end for 5 mm, and glue the two parts over each other. Round the points or curves with your quill pen.
Glue the shapes (2 × 5) overlapping each other and glue 1 tight coil in the centre. Attach 3 leaves below or above the flower.

16: Folded roses (see page 11).

17: Make 12 loops.
Glue 4 loops together as upright as possible.
Glue the next 4 loops under the first 4, pointing out between them. Glue the final 4 loops pointing straight out under the first 4 loops.

18: Glue 6 ovals (12 cm) with the points together. 1 tight circle (6 cm) on top.

19: Glue five 3 cm dark strips to five 8 cm light strips. Starting at the light ends, make 5 teardrops, and glue them to a tight circle (5 cm) of the dark colour. Glue 5 teardrops (8 cm) as leaves to an 8 cm strip.

Turn back to page 14 for remaining instructions.

Approx. 1.5 mm = ¹⁄₁₆″; 7 mm = ¼″; 1 cm = ⅓″; 2 cm = ¾″; 3 cm = 1¼″; 4 cm = 1½″; 5 cm = 2″; 6 cm = 2½″; 8 cm = 3″; 9 cm = 3½″; 10 cm = 4″; 12 cm = 5″; 15 cm = 6″

Flower varieties

Flower alphabet

Use 3 mm width paper for all letters unless another width is specified.

When combining letters to form a word you may wish to change the colours used in the flowers. In some the completed design is more attractive using a variety of colours—in others you may prefer to use the same colour or even the same flower for every letter. The flower design may also be changed.

First form the base of each letter using green paper on edge (see A on right). Allow for scrolls on some of the letters. The leaves, flowers and greenery are glued to this base.

All of the designs include cut out leaves. Most are cut from green paper sheets or 5 mm width paper. The grass-shaped leaves can be cut from 3 mm width paper. Vary the size of the leaves.

Cut out leaves
Cut leaves, curl slightly.
Fringed leaves
Cut leaves, fringe edges and curl slightly.
Narrow, creased leaves
Cut leaves and crease down centre. Some are straight; some are curved to fit the shape of the letter.
Grass-shaped leaves
Cut lengths of 3 mm width paper. Trim a point on one end and curl.
Variegated leaves
Cut a leaf from green paper. Cut a smaller leaf from a contrasting shade and glue to first leaf.

A
Flowers (make two): Fringe a gold 8 cm length of 5 mm width paper. Roll a 2 cm tight circle for the centre from 3 mm paper. Glue the fringed paper around the

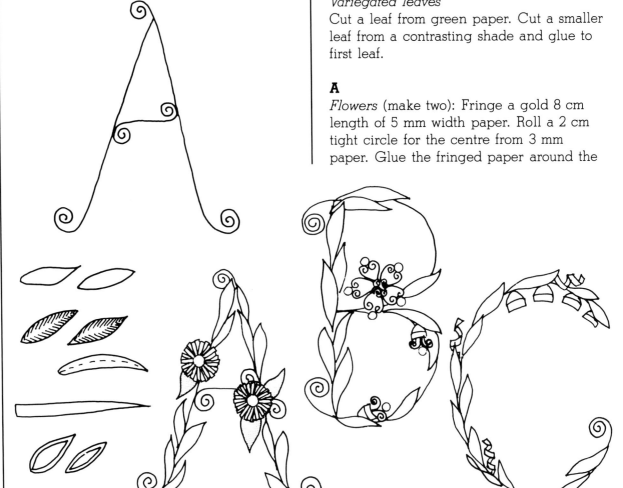

Approx. 3 mm = ⅛"; 5 mm = ¼"; 2 cm = 1"; 8 cm = 2"

tight circle and curl the fringed paper back.

Quilled leaves (shaded leaves in pattern): 3 green 8 cm teardrops of 1.5 mm paper.
Leaves: Cut 12 green fringed leaves.

B

Flower: Glue 5 lilac 5 cm open hearts together. Glue a lilac 2 cm loose circle to each open heart. For the flower centre glue 3 or 4 yellow 2 cm loose scrolls of 1.5 mm paper in a cluster (do not glue the ends of these short scrolls—leave them loose).
Buds (make 2): Glue a lilac 5 cm V scroll and a 2 cm loose circle together. Glue the point of the V scroll into a green 6 cm grape roll.
Leaves: Cut 13 green fringed leaves.

C

Flowers: Roll 2 coral 12 cm grape rolls and 2 coral 8 cm grape rolls using 1.5 mm paper. Glue to the top of the C with the larger ones in the centre.
Leaves: Cut 14 green fringed leaves. Add 3 short green spirals of 1.5 mm paper as greenery.

D

Flowers: Roll 7 pale pink 6 cm fringed flowers from 5 mm paper.
Leaves: Cut 12 green narrow creased leaves. Cut some curved to follow the line of the curved section of the D. Add several curled narrow slivers of paper as greenery.

E

Flowers (make 8): Glue together 3 sky blue 5 cm teardrops of 1.5 mm paper. Do not glue these petals flat—glue together at an angle so the flower is cup-shaped. Add a deep blue 2 cm tight circle of 1.5 mm paper for the centre.
Leaves: Cut 17 green fringed leaves.

F

Flowers: Roll 10 pink 6 cm flower petals.
Leaves: Cut 9 green narrow creased leaves. These leaves are slightly curved.

G

Flower: Roll 5 ivory 5 cm teardrops. Add 1 loop of cadet blue to outline each teardrop. Glue these 5 petals together and add a deep blue 5 cm tight circle of 1.5 mm paper for the centre.
Bud: Glue a cadet blue 5 cm teardrop into a green 5 cm grape roll made with narrow paper.
Leaves: Cut 14 green fringed leaves.

Approx. 1.5 mm = ¹⁄₁₆″; 5 mm = ¼″; 2 cm = ¾″; 5 cm = 2″; 6 cm = 3″; 8 cm = 3″; 12 cm = 5″

Flower alphabet

H

Buds (make 6): Roll a deep red 2.5 cm tight closed spiral on the tool (◁—▭). Spread glue inside so it will retain its shape. Cut 4 or 5 short lengths of green paper with points on both ends. Glue these to form calyx. Curl the top ends out from the bud. Glue the bottom ends together.
Leaves: Cut 11 green fringed leaves.

I

Flower: Glue 2 red 8 cm narrow marquises to a red narrow 10 cm teardrop using 1.5 mm paper. Glue these into a green 8 cm grape roll, adding 4 or 5 slivers of green paper for the calyx. Curl the calyx back.
Leaves: Cut 2 green long cutout leaves.

J

Flower: Roll 8 apricot 5 cm tight closed spirals on the tool (◁—▭). Spread glue inside so they will retain their shape. Glue these to the top of the J with the centre overlapping the side spirals.
Leaves: Cut 10 variegated leaves using soft green on green.

K

Flower: Glue together 5 red 5 cm teardrops and add a coral 4 cm inverted grape roll using 1.5 mm paper.

Buds (make 2): Glue a red 8 cm teardrop into a green 5 cm grape roll (1.5 mm paper).
Leaves: Cut 9 fringed leaves.

L

Flowers (make 2): Glue together 4 bright yellow 8 cm bunny ears and add a gold 4 cm loose circle using 1.5 mm paper for the centre.
Leaves: Cut 5 green fringed leaves.

M

Flowers: Roll 5 turquoise 8 cm fringed flowers from 3 mm paper.
Leaves: Cut 13 variegated leaves using soft green on green.

Approx. 1.5 mm = 1/16″; 4 cm = 2″; 8 cm = 3″; 10 cm = 4″

22

N

Flowers (make 2): Roll a deep red 8 cm V scroll. Cut 3 pink 1 cm lengths. Fold these pink lengths into V shapes, fringe the ends and glue into the V scroll. Glue these 2 flowers to the top of the N.
Leaves: Cut 18 green grass-shaped leaves.

O

Flower: Glue together 5 lilac 5 cm teardrops. For the flower centre glue 3 or 4 yellow 1 cm loose scrolls of 1.5 mm paper in a cluster (do not glue the ends of these short scrolls—leave them loose).
Buds (make 2): Glue a lilac 5 cm teardrop into a green 5 cm grape roll using 1.5 mm paper.
Leaves: Cut 18 green fringed leaves.

P

Flowers (make 3): Roll an orange 8 cm fringed flower using 7 mm paper.
Quilled leaves (shaded leaves in pattern): 7 green 10 cm marquises.
Leaves: Cut 8 green fringed leaves.

Q

Flowers: Roll 3 pale pink 5 cm open hearts.
Leaves: Cut 15 variegated leaves using soft green on green.

R

Flowers (make 5): Cut a 4 cm length of 1.5 mm bright yellow paper—fold off-centre so one end is 2.5 cm and one is 1.5 cm and roll a scroll on each end.
Leaves: Cut 7 green fringed leaves. Add narrow curled slivers of green as greenery.

S

Flowers (make 2): Using 1.5 mm paper, glue together 4 yellow 3 cm open hearts. Add a cadet blue 4 cm tight circle for centre.
Leaves: Cut 12 green fringed leaves.

T

Flowers (make 3): Fringe a 6 cm length of 5 mm red paper. Roll an ivory 6 cm tight circle of 1.5 mm paper. Glue the fringed paper around the tight circle and curl the fringed paper back.

Leaves: Cut 10 green fringed leaves. Add 2 short green spirals of 1.5 mm paper as greenery.

U

Flowers: Roll 6 gold 4 cm tight closed spirals on the tool (⟶◁—▭). Spread glue inside so they will retain their shape. Glue 3 to each end of the U with the centre spiral overlapping the side spirals.

Leaves: Cut 14 green fringed leaves.

V

Flowers (make 3): Roll a cadet blue 5 cm fringed flower using 5 mm paper. Glue into a green 5 cm grape roll made with 1.5 mm paper.

Leaves: Cut 9 green grass-shaped leaves.

W

Flowers (make 3): Glue together 3 orange 5 cm teardrops of 1.5 mm paper. Do not glue the petals flat—glue them at an angle so the flower is cup-shaped. Add an apricot 3 cm tight circle of 1.5 mm paper for the centre.

Leaves: Cut 15 green fringed leaves.

X

Flowers: Roll 19 turquoise 3 cm teardrops of 1.5 mm paper. Glue these together as in pattern.

Leaves: Cut 10 green narrow creased leaves.

Y

Flowers (make 3): Glue a lilac 3 cm teardrop into a cadet blue 3 cm V scroll.

Leaves: Cut 10 green grass-shaped leaves.

Z

Flowers (make 2): Glue together 5 orange 6 cm teardrops for the petal and add a coral 4 cm tight circle using 1.5 mm paper for the centre.

Leaves: Cut 9 green fringed leaves.

Approx. 1.5 mm = ¹⁄₁₆″; 5 mm = ¼″; 1 cm = ½″; 2.5 cm = 1″; 3 cm = 1¼″; 4 cm = 1½″; 5 cm = 2″; 6 cm = 2½″; 8 cm = 3″; 10 cm = 4″

Panda

Panda

Trace the drawing from the book onto
tracing paper, each part separately. Lay
the drawing on top of a piece of strong
cardboard or foam. Cover with clear
plastic lunch wrap or transparent wax
paperwhich is firmly attached to the back
of the cardboard or foam.

Start making a large number of white and
black marquises (12 cm). Store them
separately in small boxes.

Then make eyes, nose and tongue and
secure them with pins on the appropriate
places on the outline. Make two grape rolls
of 30 cm for the eyes. The centres must be
tight. Around the eyes glue a 10 cm white
strip. Pin the eyes on their places on the
drawing.

Glue black marquises around the eyes.
These marquises must be reworked one by
one to the desired shape, and glued
immediately. Start with the marquise
closest to the nose. Curve it around the
eye, with the convex side towards the
outline. Glue the shape to the eye
and fix with pins. Glue more
black marquises around the
eye, following the outline.
Sometimes you may need
to make a triangle shape to fit
properly. At the cheek sides the
shapes have to point out to get the
panda eye shape. Use enough pins
to prevent the shapes moving.

Nose
Make the nose from a fairly tight
black circle which is still loose
enough to be formed into a
triangle. This triangle must
be pushed out a bit in the
centre like a grape roll.

Pattern for panda

Make a fold in a black 2 cm strip and bow
the ends a bit. Glue it with the fold under
the nose. Make a pink triangle of 8 cm and
glue it in the angle formed by the black
strip. Fix nose and mouth with pins.

Now start with the upper edge of the head
with white marquises. Occasionally the

Approx. 2 cm = ¾″; 8 cm = 3″; 10 cm = 4″;
12 cm = 5″; 30 cm = 12″

marquises must be reshaped to fit the design's outline, particularly around the eye, nose and mouth. For this reason they should not be rolled too tightly. Glue the first two marquises together at the points. Fix them with pins on the upper outline.

Put some glue on the third shape and position it with a pin between the two others.

The next shapes are fixed between the points of the previous ones. Make sure that they are close together.

When the head is finished, turn the pins and pull them out. Use a flat knife to lift the head from the drawing. Store it in a box until the rest is finished.

Body

Start the body in the same way as the head. Fill it in with lines of white marquises. Glue them as vertical as possible to get a beautiful lined effect.

Legs and ears

Legs and ears are made of black marquises. Because they are smaller, you will have to reshape them more frequently then you had to do with the head and body. Doing this is not difficult if the marquises are not rolled too tightly.

Greenery

The greenery is made of pointed green strips, folded lengthwise. Bow the upper part of the strips and glue 3 or 4 strips together.

Background

When the shapes are finished start making the background. Take a mat board (35 × 25 cm) and cover it with striped material. Frame it with a 2 cm high frame, covered with the same material.

Assembly

Mark the places for the different pieces of the panda with a pencil.

Take the parts one by one in the palm of your hand and push them carefully into a concave shape. Don't forget the legs and ears.

Glue the right legs to the background first. Then glue the body over them. By glueing the right side first and then the left side, you can arch the body more.

Glue on the head next, first positioning the right ear under the head. Then glue the left ear on a slant onto the head. Now glue the left legs on the body and arrange the greenery.

You don't have to use leaves—you can let the panda hold something else such as a heart, a note or a diploma. There are many possibilities for an original and very personal present.

Finally the completed, covered frame is covered with glass and a wooden frame 3.5 cm deep. On the back you can fix a cardboard plate and a hanger.

Approx. 2 cm = ¾"; 3.5 cm = 1¼";
35 × 25 cm = 14" × 10"

Pansies (illustrated on page 2)

The flowers are made of 1.5 mm strips. This width makes bending the petals easier and gives a very delicate appearance.

Flowers

Fix the drawing on your quilling board. Using the photograph on page 6 as a guide, make the centre of the flower from a tight black circle (10 cm). The half-moons on the inner edge of the petals are bright yellow (5 cm). Then glue some purple marquises to the yellow ones. Fill in the shape with yellow marquises (10 cm). Sometimes you have to reshape the marquises to follow the outline. Make all the petals. Gently curve and shape each petal in your hand. Then glue them together.

Buds

Make three bright yellow petals from strips 7.5, 10 and 15 cm long and glue them together. Make several narrow, pointed, curled strips of green for the calyx and glue around the base, overlapping each other. Make a green grape roll (15 cm) and glue over the bud.

Leaves

For each leaf make 8 marquises (green, 12 cm) and glue them together, then curve and shape slightly.

Stems

Curved double strips.

Patterns for pansies

Approx. 1.5 mm = ¹⁄₁₆″; 5 cm = 2″; 7.5 cm = 3″; 10 cm = 4″; 12 cm = 5″; 15 cm = 6″

Poppies

Poppies

Fix the drawing on your quilling board.

Flowers

Petals: Fill in patterns with red marquises (8 cm long, 1.5 mm wide). Curve each petal gently and glue together, overlapping each other.

Centres: Make a black grape roll (15 cm). Fringe the ends of 2 soft green 2 cm strips, then cross and glue as in pattern. Glue the centre to the back of the grape roll and curl ends over the grape roll. Fringe the edges of 4 black 3 cm strips, then cross and glue. Glue the centre to the back of the grape roll and small fringe and curl edges up slightly. Glue in the centre of the petals.

Buds

1. (Make 2): Make 3 green and 1 red marquises (25 cm), rolled rather tightly. Glue them together with the red one in the centre.
2. (Make 2): Make 3 red marquises (25 cm) and glue them together. Cut 5 small green leaves from a 7 mm wide strip and glue them around the red marquises. Make 4 grape rolls (8 cm) and glue the buds into them.

Leaves

11 green marquises (10 cm) per leaf.

Stems

Double curved strips (1.5 mm).

Patterns for poppy flowers

Approx. 1.5 mm = ⅟₁₆″; 7 mm = ¼″; 2 cm = ¾″; 3 cm = 1¼″; 8 cm = 3″; 10 cm = 4″; 15 cm = 6″; 25 cm = 10″

Fantastic bird

Wing (make two)
Teardrops:
3 light blue (20 cm)
2 blue (20 cm)
2 jade green (20 cm)
Short scrolls:
2 light blue
4 blue
3 jade green
Long scrolls:
3 light blue
1 blue
1 jade green
Make the lengths of the scrolls to your own taste.

Body
Eye: tight circle (2.5 cm black with 5 cm white) rolled inside a 7.5 cm blue triangle
Crest: loose scroll:
1 light blue (3 cm)
1 blue (3 cm)
1 jade green (3 cm)
Body: marquises:
12 blue (7.5 cm)

Tail
Long scrolls:
6 blue
3 jade green
4 light blue

Exotic flowers

First layer
Long scrolls of pale pink, as in the pattern, glued in the centre.

Second layer
Add mid-pink scrolls, with several of pale pink and rose scattered throughout.
Graduate from long scrolls nearly horizontal on the ends to shorter, vertical scrolls in the centre.
Add 5 green 1 cm pointed lengths under the flower head for calyx.
The flowers are finished with fringed leaves cut from green paper.

The branches are made of multiple strips of paper straight from the packet, glued at both ends. If you want to frame this design, the ends of the branches can be worked behind the frame.

Approx. 1 cm = ½"; 2.5 cm = 1"; 3 cm = 1¼"; 5 cm = 2"; 7.5 cm = 3"; 20 cm = 8"

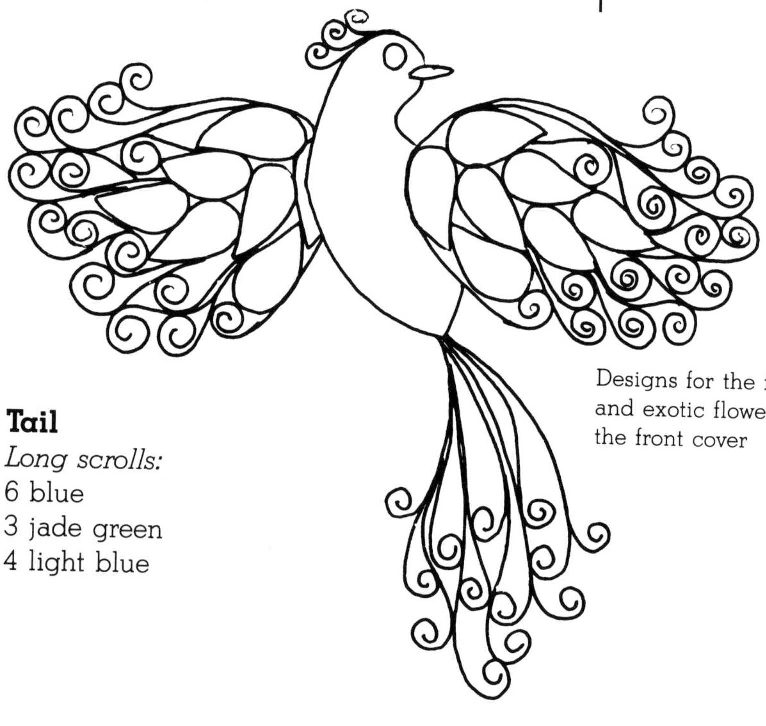

Designs for the fantastic bird and exotic flowers shown on the front cover

Christmas bells and stars

Christmas bells

Bells:
7 scrolls (10 cm)
8 marquises (10 cm)
6 closed hearts (10 cm)
2 loose circles (8 cm)
6 loose circles (5 cm)
Enough marquises to fill up the bell shape.
Clappers: 6 teardrops (10 cm)

Trace the design from page 33 onto white paper and fix it on your quilling board. Start by making the base of the bell. Fasten shapes with pins to paper design. Then fill in the rest of the shape (glueing the pieces together carefully). Follow the outline accurately.

Approx. 5 cm = 2″; 8 cm = 3″; 10 cm = 4″; 12 cm = 5″

When the bell is finished pull out the pins carefully, take the bell in the palm of your hand and press it into a convex shape. Glue the clappers to the underside.

Christmas stars

Using the photographs on the next page as a guide, draw a circle 5 cm in diameter and place it on the quilling board. Divide it into six parts. Place pins as shown and run a long strip of paper around the pins as a guide for making the star.

Big star
Start glueing from the centre.
6 open hearts (12 cm)
6 spirals (length 5 cm). Roll silver and white strips together

Christmas bells

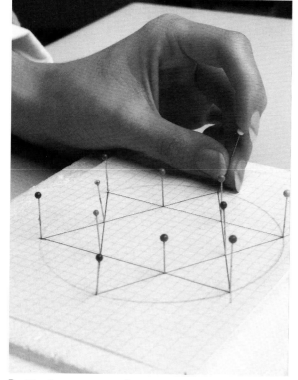

Positioning pins on a diagram

6 spirals (length 3 cm). Roll silver and
white strips together
12 marquises (12 cm)
24 S scrolls (12 cm)
6 V scrolls (12 cm)

6 marquises (12 cm with 3 cm silver glued
at the end)
6 teardrops (12 cm with 3 cm silver glued
at the end)

Star with loops
Make 36 loops (white, 5 mm width).
Glue 6 loops together, pointing out, to
make the centre of the star. Then glue 6
groups of 4 loops with points inside each
other. Glue these into the six points of the
centre. Make 6 tight spirals (12 cm). Glue
a loop in the open end, then glue between
the other points.

Star with crimped edge
Instructions for milling (or crimping) paper
are given on page 14.

Draw a star with 4 points and fix it on your
quilling board. Position 8 pins in the
corners, as shown in the photograph. Glue
4 layers of paper around the pins. Then
add a crimped strip. Cut it at the points.
Add another layer of smooth paper and
then another milled (crimped) one. Finish
with a smooth layer.

Approx. 5 mm = ³⁄₁₆″; 3 cm = 1¼″; 12 cm = 5″

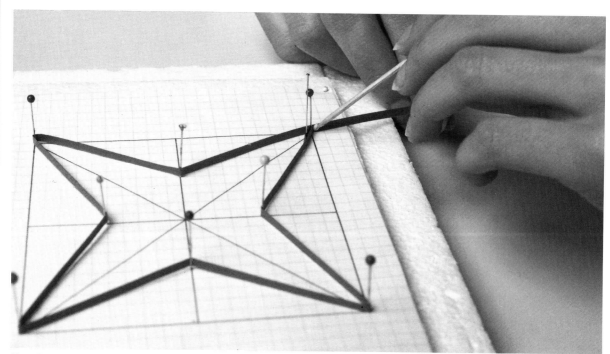

Attaching the strips. Apply glue to the corners

Christmas stars

Make 24 loops.
Glue 4 loops together in a cross (points to
the centre), then 4 loops pointing out. On
top glue 4 loops pointing out, and more
upright. Glue 4 loops on the out-pointing
second layer.

This star has to fit inside the four points of
the star made from crimped paper. Glue
the two stars together, then glue 4 pairs of
loops on the outside of the star.

Pattern for the Christmas bell

Picture alphabet

Picture alphabet

The wording on this sampler was made from rub-down lettering available in art and some craft shops. Many different typefaces are available.

The background is divided into 28 equal parts. You can glue down coloured paper for a chequerboard effect, as here. Mark the positions for the letters lightly with pencil. When the letters are on their places, you can glue 1.5 mm strips over the lines between them if you wish.

Use 3 mm width paper for the designs unless another width is specified.

Apple
Fill in outline of apple with approximately 17 red 8 cm marquises. Add a short length of brown paper for the stem and 2 green 8 cm marquises for leaves.

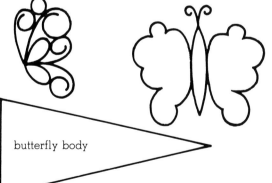

butterfly body

Butterfly
Body: Cut the butterfly body from a piece of gold paper. Roll from wide end and glue the point. Roll straight; the point should be in the exact centre when rolled.
Wings (make 2): Roll one yellow 5 cm loose scroll, one yellow 8 cm teardrop, one yellow 5 cm teardrop, one gold 4 cm loose circle, 2 gold 5 cm loose scrolls and one gold 8 cm loose scroll. Glue the wing together following the pattern with the yellow 5 cm scroll nearest the body.
Assembly of butterfly: Glue the wings to the body at slight angles so the outer edges of the wings are elevated. Roll a V scroll of a short length of narrow black paper and glue to the body as antennae.

Clock
Cut a 2.25 cm diameter circle from gold paper for the clock face. Print numbers around the edge and draw the two hands. Roll 10 brown 5 cm marquises and glue in a circle to the edge of the clock face. Cut two 7.5 mm × 15 mm rectangles from gold paper and roll into tight circles. Attach these to clock with short strips of narrow brown paper.

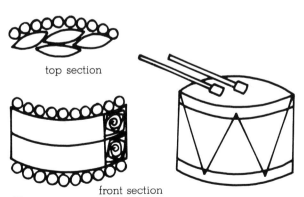

top section

front section

Drum
Top section: Glue 10 red 5 cm tight circles together for rim. Add 4 tan 8 cm marquises.
Front section: The centre is made of 10 cadet blue 8 cm squares with 10 red 5 cm tight circles glued along top edge and 10

Approx. 1.5 mm = ¹⁄₁₆″; 3 mm = ⅛″; 2.25 cm = ⅞″; 4 cm = 1½″; 5 cm = 2″; 8 cm = 3″; 7.5 × 15 mm = ¼″ × ½″

red 5 cm tight circles glued along bottom edge. Add 4 spirals of narrow black paper to front of drum as tension rods. Glue front section to top section following dotted lines as in pattern.

Drumsticks: Cut two 3 cm lengths of 3 mm wide dowel and glue a short length of white paper tightly around one end of each stick.

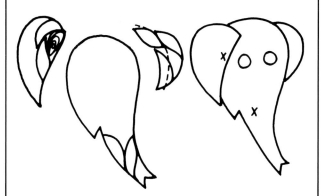

Elephant

Head: Fill in outline with approximately 19 grey 5 cm marquises and half moons.

Ears: Glue 4 grey 5 cm marquises together for back ear. Fill in outline of front ear with 7 grey 5 cm marquises and half moons.

Eyes: Two orange 8 cm tight circles.

Assembly of elephant: Glue back ear behind head and front ear to head. Add eyes. Glue 2 pegs (tight circles used to elevate a design) behind head in the positions marked X.

Fan

Cut six 3 cm lengths of raspberry paper. These are glued on edge with a pink 5 cm open heart and a pink 5 cm S scroll between each length of raspberry paper. Fringe 3 or 4 short lengths of pink paper and add to point of fan for a tassel.

Grapes

Roll 20 lilac 5 cm loose circles. Glue 14 together for the lower layer and add 6 for the top layer. Roll 2 loose spirals for the tendrils, using short lengths of narrow width brown paper. Add 3 green 10 cm bunny ears for the leaves.

crown

brim

Hat

Crown: Fill in outline with seven 5 cm marquises, using bright yellow narrow width paper.

Brim: Glue together eight 8 cm bunny ears and seven 8 cm teardrops made of bright yellow narrow width paper. Gently shape brim so that it curves out and glue to crown.

Trim: Add a length of gold paper for the hat band and 2 short lengths of gold as streamers. Roll a cadet blue 8 cm fringed flower and glue to hat.

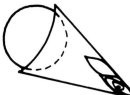

Ice cream cone

Ice cream: Roll a 120 cm pink grape roll (glue two 60 cm lengths together end to end).

Cone: Fill in outline of cone with ten 5 cm marquises and three 5 cm triangles, using tan narrow width paper. Gently curve cone and glue to ice cream.

Jack-o-lantern

Pumpkin: Fill in outline with approximately 16 orange 8 cm marquises and half moons.

Face: Roll 3 black 5 cm triangles and a

Approx. 3 mm = ⅛″; 3 cm = 1¼″; 5 cm = 2″; 8 cm = 3″; 10 cm = 4″; 60 cm = 24″; 120 cm = 48″

black 10 cm marquise.
Stem: Green 5 cm teardrop.

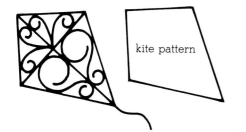

kite pattern

Kite

Cut background from a piece of deep blue paper. Glue strips of red paper on edge for cross pieces and tail. Add 2 red 5 cm V scrolls and 2 red 8 cm S scrolls as in pattern.

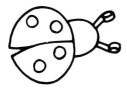

Ladybug

Body: Roll 2 red 30 cm loose circles and shape into irregular half circles as in wing patterns. Add four 5 cm tight circles using narrow width black paper for the spots.
Head: Roll a black 15 cm half circle and add two 3 cm loose scrolls made with narrow width black paper.

Mouse

Body: Roll a grey 30 cm marquise.
Head: Roll a grey 12 cm marquise.
Ear: Roll a pink 8 cm teardrop and glue a length of grey paper around the teardrop.
Nose: Roll a black 5 cm tight circle.
Foot: Roll a black 4 cm teardrop.
Tail: Roll a grey 8 cm loose scroll.

Nest

Nest: Roll a tan 120 cm grape roll (glue two 60 cm lengths of paper together end to end). Cover outside with short spirals of tan narrow width paper.
Eggs: Roll 3 cadet blue 23 cm grape rolls.
Branch: Roll lengths of brown paper into spirals.
Leaves: Roll 5 green 5 cm teardrops.

lower layer

completed owl

Owl

Lower layer: For the body roll eight 5 cm tight circles and make each wing with a brown 8 cm marquise and a brown 8 cm half moon. Cut feet from a piece of gold paper, fold on the dotted line and glue to body. For the head first roll a brown 5 cm tight circle, 2 brown 5 cm teardrops and a brown 5 cm marquise and glue together. For each eye glue together a brown 5 cm length and a tan 5 cm length and roll into a tight circle, beginning with the brown end.
Top layer: The crown is a gold 5 cm tight circle and 2 short spirals made with gold narrow width paper. Glue these to the tight circle directly above the eyes. Roll a beak of a 5 cm teardrop of gold narrow width paper and glue just below the eyes.
Branch: Roll a brown spiral for the branch and add 2 green 5 cm teardrops for leaves.

Peas

Fill in outlines of the two sections of the hull with 5 cm marquises of green narrow width paper. For the peas roll 2 spring green 23 cm grape rolls and 2 spring green 18 cm grape rolls. Glue the peas to the wider section of the hull with the larger

Approx. 4 cm = 1½"; 5 cm = 2"; 8 cm = 3"; 10 cm = 4"; 15 cm = 6"; 18 cm = 7"; 23 cm = 9"; 60 cm = 24"; 120 cm = 48"

width paper for the eyes. Glue head to body.

Ears: For each ear glue a pink 5 cm length and a white 6.5 cm length together end to end. Roll a teardrop beginning with the pink end and glue to head.

Feet: Roll 2 white 6.5 cm teardrops and glue to body.

Arms: Roll 2 white 5 cm teardrops. Glue both to body with one tilted so it can hold a flower.

Flower: Make petals with 3 tiny petals of 3 cm teardrops, using cadet blue narrow width paper. Glue together and add a stem of a short length of green narrow width paper. Glue flower stem to tilted arm.

ones in the centre. Gently round and shape the upper part of the hull and glue in place. Add a short spiral of green narrow width paper for the stem and two 15 cm teardrops of green narrow width paper for the leaves.

Quill
Cut the quill from a gold piece of paper, draw a line down the centre and fringe the edge. Glue together 3 grey 8 cm triangles and add a grey 5 cm rectangle to the top for the inkwell.

Sailboat
Fill in outlines of each sail with white 5 cm marquises. Roll spirals of black paper for the mast and boom. Glue mainsail to mast and boom. Gently round jib so it billows out and glue to mast. Glue a peg (tight circle used to elevate design) under the jib at the X. The hull is made of 2 red 5 cm triangles and 2 red 5 cm squares. Glue the hull together and glue to mast.

Rabbit
Body: Roll a tight circle of a 90 cm length of white paper (glue a 60 cm length and a 30 cm length together end to end).

Head: Roll a white 50 cm tight circle. Cut a 1.5 cm length of tan narrow width paper and fringe both ends. Glue a 3 cm tight circle of tan narrow width paper to the centre of this length of tan paper. Glue these to the head as the nose and whiskers. Roll two 3 cm tight circles of pink narrow

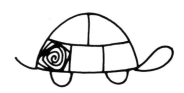

Turtle
For the shell glue together 5 gold 10 cm lengths to 5 brown 5 cm lengths end to end. Roll these into the 5 irregular shaped squares and triangles pictured in the pattern. Begin each roll with the gold end of the paper. The feet are 2 brown 5 cm half circles. Roll a brown 8 cm teardrop for the head. The tail is a short length of brown paper.

Approx. 1.5 cm = ½″; 3 cm = 1¼″; 5 cm = 2″; 6.5 cm = 2½″; 8 cm = 4″; 10 cm = 5″; 60 cm = 24″; 90 cm = 36″

Umbrella

Roll 5 red 8 cm bunny ears. Roll 5 red teardrops—one 8 cm, two 13 cm and two 17.5 cm. Glue these together following the pattern, with a length of red paper glued on edge between each section. Add a black 3 cm tight circle to top and a black spiral for handle.

Violet

Glue together 5 lilac 8 cm teardrops and add a gold 5 cm tight circle for the flower centre. Each bud is made by glueing a lilac 8 cm teardrop and 2 green 5 cm marquises together. The stems are short lengths of green paper and the leaf is a green 15 cm teardrop.

Wheat

Roll 13 tan 8 cm marquises. Glue a short pointed length of tan narrow width paper to one end of each marquise. Glue these together in two layers following pattern. Add lengths of tan paper as stems.

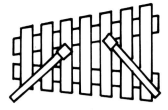

Xylophone

Base: Make 2 rows of 6 black 5 cm marquises.
Keys: The 7 keys are lengths of paper glued to the base in this order, beginning on the left: red, orange, yellow, gold, green, blue, lilac.
Mallets: Cut two 2 cm lengths of 3 mm dowel and glue short lengths of white paper tightly around end.

Yarn

Glue three 60 cm lengths of cadet blue narrow width paper end to end and loop together as in drawing. Cut a 2 cm × 3 cm rectangle from gold paper. Print the words FINE KNITTING YARN on the rectangle. Wrap rectangle around the yarn and glue ends together.

Zinnia

Centre: Glue 7 gold 5 cm tight circles together.
Petals: Roll six 15 cm teardrops and eight 13 cm teardrops using bright yellow narrow width paper. Glue the 15 cm teardrops to the flower centre for the lower layer of petals. Glue the 13 cm teardrops to the flower centre for the top layer. These teardrops are glued at a slight angle so the points are elevated.

Approx. 3 cm = 1¼"; 5 cm = 2"; 8 cm = 3"; 13 cm = 5"; 15 cm = 6"; 17.5 cm = 6½"; 60 cm = 24";
2 × 3 cm = ¾" × 1¼"

Flower basket

Flower basket

Weaving

The flower basket on the facing page is made of plaited strips. Mat-plaiting is quite easy to do. Pretty variations can be made with different colours and widths of paper.

Make a drawing of the shape you prefer. Then cut strips to fill the shape, making them 4 cm (1½″) longer than the pattern width. Working over squared paper (to help you stay straight), fix the longest strip with pins at one side of the paper. (To ensure that the strips remain parallel and do not move you need to use two pins in every strip.) Leave the other end loose.

Now plait the first cross-strip through. Under every upper strip you put a very tiny spot of glue (see lower picture). Go on like this until the weaving is large enough. Allow to dry, then pull all the pins out of your workboard.

Draw the pattern shape on the back of the mat, and cut out. Glue onto your chosen

background, arching the basket slightly and leaving the top edge unglued to allow the positioning of flower stalks and the handle. The handle is made of a long spiral.

You can follow the arrangement pictured for the bouquet in the basket, or make one to your own design. Sometimes you may need to glue some extra scrolls under the flowers to add depth to the arrangement.

Making a spiral

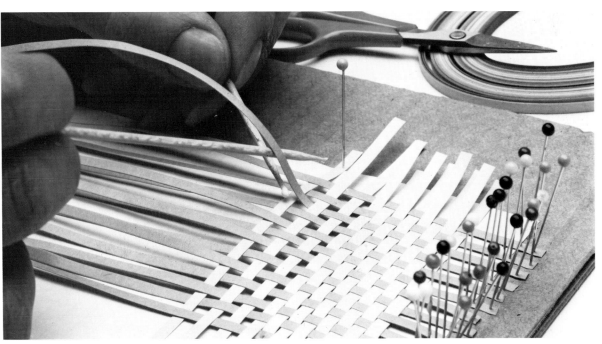

Applying glue

25
years

What use is
good fortune
if you can't share it
with friends?

Oval cards

Oval cards

Sometimes you see or hear a saying that catches your attention, of which you say: 'That's a good one, I should remember it.' Or you graduate, get a birth announcement, read a beautiful poem. All things worth saving.

Framed, such things can make an original present, or something you might like to keep for yourself. Write the text on a piece of paper. If your handwriting is not so wonderful you can use rub-down lettering.

Upper oval
1 pink flower of 6 ovals (22 cm)
1 pink flower of 5 ovals (20 cm)
1 pink flower of 9 flower petals (6 of 15 cm and 3 of 10 cm)
All these flowers have a dark pink 5 cm tight circle at the centre.
6 dark pink fringed flowers (10 cm × 7 mm wide)
4 pink fringed flowers with tight circles as a centre (5 cm × 3 mm and pink fringed strip 8 cm × 7 mm wide)
3 light tan flowers of 5 teardrops (6 cm × 3 mm wide with a tight circle of light tan 3 mm × 1.5 mm at the centre)
10 light green scrolls
14 fringed leaves (dark green)
10 fringed leaves (light green)
Arrange the flowers and leaves on the edge of the oval mat.

Lower oval
Make 3 white flowers each of 14 ovals (20 cm). Glue 7 ovals in a ring with an open centre. When glue is dry, round it in the palm of your hand, then glue the next 7 ovals on the top of it. The centre is made of a white grape roll (15 cm with 2 cm green on the outside).

Make 5 white flowers each of 5 ovals (12 cm). Glue a few green scrolls on the centre (2 cm × 1.5 mm wide).

Fourteen green leaves, made by glueing 5 looped strips (2, 3 and 4 cm) together.

Arrange the flowers and leaves above and below the oval mat.

Approx. 3 mm = ⅛"; 7 mm = ½"; 2 cm = ¾";
3 cm = 1¼"; 4 cm = 1½"; 5 cm = 2"; 6 cm = 2½";
8 cm = 3"; 10 cm = 4"; 12 cm = 5"; 15 cm = 6";
20 cm = 8"; 22 cm = 8¾"

44

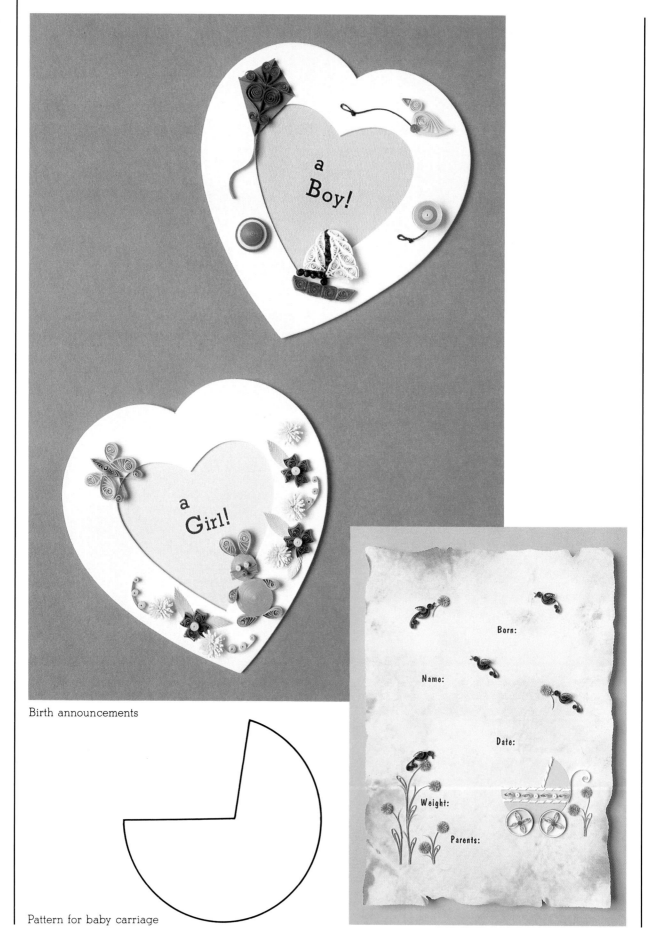

Birth announcements

Pattern for baby carriage

Birth announcements

A boy!

Boat

Hull: 4 red 10 cm squares.
Mast and boom: 12 black 4 cm tight circles.
Sails: 8 cm marquises (white), 7 for front sail and 5 for rear. Glue a peg (tight circle used to elevate design) under the jib.

Yo-yo

Front: 13 cm light blue, 24 cm grey-blue and 50 cm light blue glued end-to-end and rolled into a tight circle, beginning with the 13 cm light blue.
Back: light blue 86 cm tight circle.

Ball

60 cm blue, 30 cm yellow, and 30 cm blue, glued end-to-end and rolled into a tight circle, beginning with the 60 cm blue.

Kite

2 red 7 cm V scrolls, 2 red 10 cm S scrolls, 2 strips red paper for dividers; blue background paper.

Duck

Body: yellow 30 cm teardrop.
Head: yellow 8 cm loose circle.
Wheel: red 8 cm tight circle.
Beak: red 3 cm triangle.

A girl!

Bunny

Body: 3 lengths (150 cm) tan glued end-to-end and rolled into a tight circle.
Head: tan 25 cm tight circle.
Ears: 5 cm tan and 8 cm pink glued end-to-end and rolled into teardrop, beginning with the pink.

Eyes: pink 2.5 cm tight circles.
Whiskers: 2 cm tan, fringed on edges and glued under eyes.
Nose: tan 2.5 cm tight circle, glued over centre of whiskers.
Feet: 2 tan 10 cm teardrops.
Arms: 2 tan 8 cm teardrops.

Butterfly and flowers

Make a yellow and tan butterfly following the instructions on page 35; 3 blue flower-petal flowers with centres, 5 pale yellow fringed flowers, 3 spring green bud sprays, 5 spring green fringed leaves. Flower instructions are given on page 17.

'Parchment' sampler

Bluebirds (make 5:)
1 half circle (blue 12.5 cm).
1 loose circle (blue 7.5 cm).
2 short scrolls (blue).
1 V scroll (blue 5 cm).

Fringed flowers:
9 pink fringed flowers (7.5 cm × 5 mm).
5 spring green lengths (1.5 mm width) on edge for stems
Green 1.5 mm looped for leaves.
Baby carriage:

Body: Cut from light blue according to pattern and decorate with 4 ovals (white 6 cm), 3 tight circles (white 6 cm) and 15 cm of white spiral.
Handle: long white loose scroll.
Wheels: wrap 5 layers of white paper around a form of 2 cm diameter dowel, then wrap a layer of blue around white. 4 white ovals for spokes with 1 blue tight circle at the centre.

Approx. 15 mm = $\frac{1}{16}$"; 5 mm = $\frac{1}{4}$"; 2.5 cm = 1";
3 cm = 1$\frac{1}{4}$"; 4 cm = 1$\frac{1}{2}$"; 6 cm = 2$\frac{1}{2}$"; 7 cm = 2$\frac{3}{4}$";
10 cm = 4"; 13 cm = 5$\frac{1}{4}$"; 25 cm = 10"; 30 cm = 12";
60 cm = 24"; 150 cm = 60"

Gift tags

Cheers!
Fringed flowers (5 mm width):
4 lavender (8 cm).
1 lilac (14 cm).
3 lavender (6 cm) + lilac (6 cm) duotone.
10 loose scrolls (spring green 8 cm).

Best wishes!
Bluebird:
1 V scroll (0.5 cm).
1 loose circle (6 cm).
1 half circle (20 cm).
2 teardrops (10 cm).
1 arrow (13 cm).
Flowers: 3 flowers with 5 teardrops (yellow 5 cm) and an apricot tight circle (5 cm) on the centre.
Buds: 3 buds with 1 teardrop (yellow 5 cm) and 1 V scroll (green 5 cm).
Green leaf sprays: 2 with five 5 cm ovals and 3 with three 5 cm ovals.
Green lengths for branches.

Congratulations!
Owl:
front wing: 8 teardrops (brown 5 cm)
back wing: 4 teardrops (brown 5 cm)
body: 4 teardrops (tan 5 cm)
eyes: 2 tight circles (5 cm brown and 5 cm yellow)
beak: 1 teardrop (yellow 5 cm)
head: 5 teardrops (brown 5 cm) and 2 leaves (brown 5 cm)
Diploma: tan parchment 2 × 3 cm rolled and tied with 4 cm blue strip.
Branch: brown spiral 7 cm
Leaves: 3 ovals (green 7.5 cm)

Get well soon!
Flowers:
3 flowers with 4 bunny ears (lavender 7.5 cm) and 1 loose circle (lilac 3 cm) on top of the centre.

Lilac flower sprays on green lengths, 3 with five teardrops (5 cm), 1 with three teardrops (5 cm).
5 ovals (green 7.5 cm)
5 loose scrolls (green 5 cm)

For you!
3 flat glued strips (lilac).
4 V scrolls (lilac, different lengths).
4 flower petals (pink, 6, 8, 12 cm).

For you!
Fringed flowers (5 mm width):
2 peach 8 cm
1 orange 8 cm
1 orange 6 cm and coral 6 cm duotone.
2 flowers with 5 coral 8 cm teardrops and an orange 8 cm tight circle in the centre.
Brown bud sprays:
3 with 5, 3.5 and 2 cm tight circles.
1 with 3.5 and 2 cm tight circles.
7 brown loose scrolls.

Get well soon!
3 azure clusters with three 8 cm teardrops.
1 azure cluster with five 10 cm teardrops.
4 light blue clusters with three 8 cm teardrops.
8 spring green 8 cm teardrops.
3 spring green loose scrolls.

Love!
Bird:
1 teardrop (blue 30 cm × 1.5 mm).
1 teardrop (blue 15 cm × 1.5 mm).
1 tight circle (blue 10 cm × 1.5 mm)
1 triangle (red 6 mm × 15 mm).
Letter:
1 × 1.5 cm (blue) with red strips

3 closed hearts (red 10 cm).

Approx. 5 mm = ⅜″; 2 cm = ¾″; 3 cm = 1¼″; 4 cm = 1½″; 5 cm = 2″; 6 cm = 2½″; 7 cm = 2¾″; 7.5 cm = 3″; 8 cm = 3″; 10 cm = 4″; 12 cm = 5″; 13 cm = 5½″; 20 cm = 8″

Gift tags

Christmas cards

Merry Christmas!

Make 3 candles from 15 cm strips of gold paper, 2, 2.75 and 3.5 mm wide.
3 teardrops (yellow 7 cm × 1.5 mm).
17 holly leaves (green 13 and 16 cm long × 1.5 mm wide, multipointed).
7 tight circles (red 14 cm × 1.5 mm).
Glue the holly leaves partly over each other.

Happy New Year!

Glue 4 gold strips end to end and make a tight circle, then push carefully into a bell shape. Make each clapper from a tight circle (black 4 cm × 1.5 mm) and hang it in the bell with a short strip.
15 holly leaves (13 and 16 cm long × 1.5 mm, multipointed).
5 tight circles (red 14 cm × 1.5 mm).

Approx. 2 mm = ¹⁄₁₆″; 2.75 mm = ⅛″;
3.5 mm = ³⁄₁₆″; 4 cm = 1½″;
14 cm = 5½″; 15 cm = 6″; 16 cm = 6½″

Chritmas and New Year cards